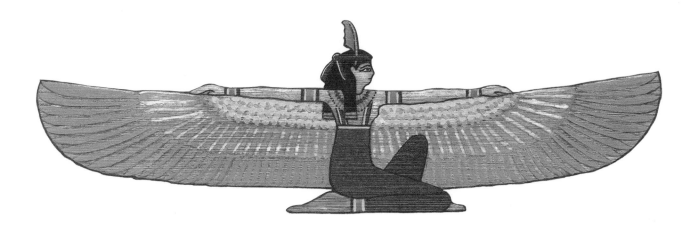

Hieroglyphs
from
A to Z

A Rhyming Book
with
Ancient Egyptian Stencils for Kids

Peter Der Manuelian

Scholastic Inc.
New York Toronto London Auckland Sydney

ISBN 0-590-40008-8

Copyright © 1991 by Peter Der Manuelian.
All rights reserved. Published by Scholastic Inc., 555 Broadway,
New York, NY 10012, by arrangement with Museum of Fine Arts, Boston.

12 11 10 9 8 7 6   8 9/9 0/0

Printed in the U.S.A.   08

First Scholastic printing, September 1995

"For my brother, David,

and his entire family"

How to Use This Book

This book shows the English alphabet from **A** to **Z**, one letter at a time. The large color hieroglyph on each of the alphabet pages shows a picture of a word that begins with the letter on that page. That's why an **A**rcher is on the **A** page and a **B**eetle on the **B** page. These large hieroglyphs are beautiful reproductions of actual ancient carvings and paintings.

At the bottom of each **A** to **Z** page is a smaller hieroglyph in a box. This is the ancient Egyptian hieroglyph that stands for the sound our English letter makes. The 𓄿 (vulture) would be read as **A**, the 𓃀 (foot) as **B**, and so on. These are the hieroglyphs you can use to spell names and words. You will find a stencil of these hieroglyphs at the back of the book.

At the back of the book you will also find a brief history of hieroglyphs and a chart to help you learn the hieroglyphs that match our alphabet.

All of the drawings are based on actual hieroglyphs that are either carved or painted on Egyptian tomb and temple walls. Many drawings come from examples on exhibit at the Museum of Fine Arts, Boston.

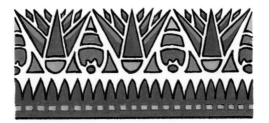

A

**is for archer
who carries a bow.**

To write the letter A the Egyptians used a vulture. To spell **archer**
using hieroglyphs, you would write

a r che e r.

The Egyptians used bows and arrows to hunt wild animals in the
desert, such as bulls, rabbits, gazelles and hedgehogs.

B

**is for beetle
whose footsteps are slow.**

To write the letter B the Egyptians used a foot. To spell **beetle** using hieroglyphs, you would write

b e e t l e.

The scarab beetle was worn as a powerful lucky charm. The Egyptians made scarab jewelry out of blue glass and jewels.

B

C

**is for cat
who sits there so still.**

The Egyptians had no letter C, but you can use a basket with handle (k) to stand for the C sound. To spell **cat** you would write

c a t.

Cats were considered sacred by the ancient Egyptians. They even had a cat goddess named Bastet.

D

**is for duck
who "quack quacks" with his bill.**

To write the letter D the Egyptians used a hand. To spell **duck** using hieroglyphs, you would write

d u ck.

The Egyptians had many of the same kinds of colorful ducks that we have today.

D

E

**is for eyes,
looking up, looking down.**

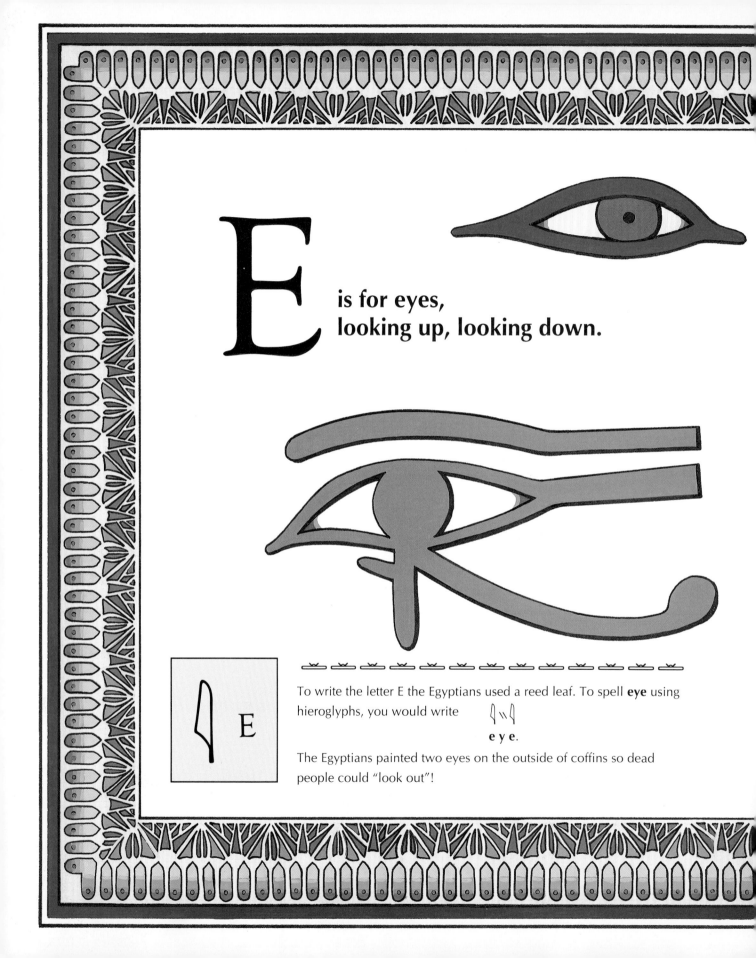

To write the letter E the Egyptians used a reed leaf. To spell **eye** using hieroglyphs, you would write

e y e.

The Egyptians painted two eyes on the outside of coffins so dead people could "look out"!

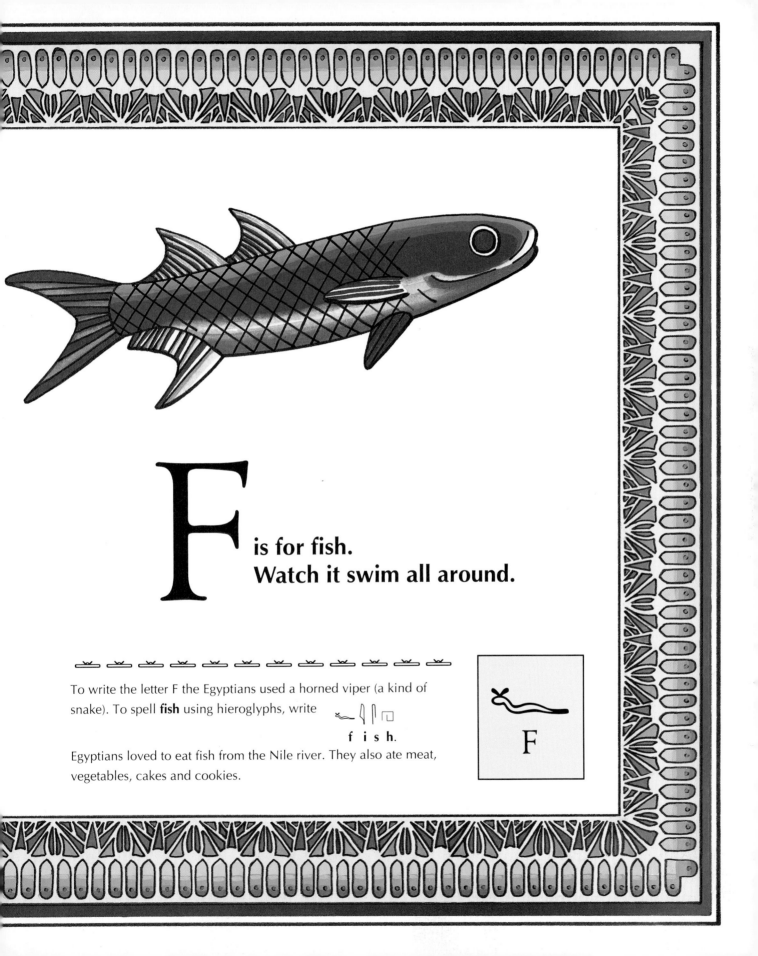

F is for fish.
Watch it swim all around.

To write the letter F the Egyptians used a horned viper (a kind of snake). To spell **fish** using hieroglyphs, write

f i s h.

Egyptians loved to eat fish from the Nile river. They also ate meat, vegetables, cakes and cookies.

F

G

**is a giraffe,
stretching high to the sky.**

To write the letter G the Egyptians used a pot stand. To spell **giraffe** using hieroglyphs, you would write

g i r a f f e.

Giraffes were rare and exotic animals that came from the land of Nubia to the south of Egypt.

H

**is a hand.
Wave your own and say "Hi!"**

To write the letter H the Egyptians used a shelter. To spell **hand** using hieroglyphs, you would write

h a n d.

Egyptian statues often show couples holding hands. Raising both hands in front of you was a sign of worship and greeting.

H

I

is for ibex.
Watch him leap out of sight.

To write the letter I the Egyptians used a reed leaf. To spell **ibex** using hieroglyphs, you would write

i b e x.

An ibex is like a mountain goat. All kinds of horned animals lived in ancient Egypt: ibexes, gazelles, oryxes and bulls.

J

**is for jackal
who prowls at night.**

To write the letter J the Egyptians used a snake. To spell **jackal** using hieroglyphs, you would write

j a ck a l.

Jackals wandered along the desert's edge near the cemeteries. Egyptians believed the jackal-headed god, Anubis, guided the dead through the Underworld.

J

K

**is for kilt
made of linen so white.**

K

To write the letter K the Egyptians used a basket with a handle. To spell **kilt** using hieroglyphs, you would write

k i l t.

Egyptian kilts were made of pleated linen. Kilts are like skirts, but they were worn by men.

L
is for lion
so proud in his might.

To write the letter L the Egyptians used a crouching lion. To spell **lion** using hieroglyphs, you would write

l i o n.

The powerful lion was a symbol for the pharaoh, or king, of Egypt. Some pharaohs even had pet lions!

L

M

**is for man
who is full of surprises.**

To write the letter M the Egyptians used an owl. To spell **man** using hieroglyphs, you would write

m a n.

Working together, thousands of men built the pyramids. The Great Pyramid has 2 1/2 million stones and took 20 years to build.

N

**is for nose
in all shapes and sizes!**

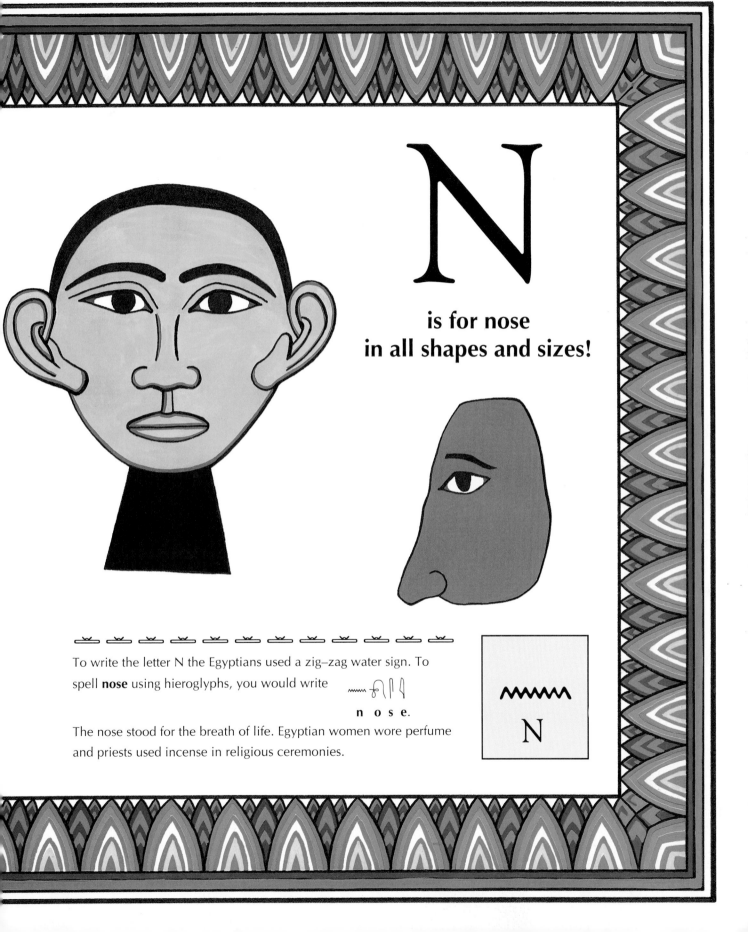

To write the letter N the Egyptians used a zig–zag water sign. To
spell **nose** using hieroglyphs, you would write

n o s e.

The nose stood for the breath of life. Egyptian women wore perfume
and priests used incense in religious ceremonies.

N

O

**is for owl
who's incredibly wise.**

To write the letter O the Egyptians used a lasso. To spell **owl** using hieroglyphs, you would write

o w l.

The Egyptians did not think the owl stood for wisdom the way we do. Its big, staring eyes reminded the Egyptians of seeing.

P

**is a pyramid,
reaching the skies.**

To write the letter P the Egyptians used a footstool. To spell **pyramid**
using hieroglyphs, you would write

p y r a m i d.

The Egyptians built pyramids to be final resting places for their kings.
The Great Pyramid is 450 feet high—almost twice as tall as the
Statue of Liberty!

P

Q

**is for quail chick,
all ready to grow.**

To write the letter Q the Egyptians used a hill. To spell **quail chick** using hieroglyphs, you would write

q u a i l   ch i ck.

Quails and many other birds—falcons, ibises, herons, lapwings, swallows, ducks and geese—lived on the banks of the Nile river.

R

is for rabbit.
Make a move—
off he'll go!

To write the letter R the Egyptians used a mouth. To spell **rabbit** using hieroglyphs, you would write

r a b b i t.

Wild rabbits lived in the Egyptian desert. One particular area in Upper Egypt worshipped a rabbit goddess named Wenut.

R

S

**is for snake,
creeping silently 'round.**

To write the letter S the Egyptians used a folded cloth. To spell **snake** using hieroglyphs, you would write   **s n a k e**.

The pharaoh wore a gold cobra on his crown as a symbol of royalty and power. The snake Meret-seger was the goddess of silence.

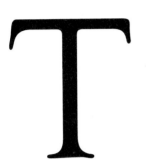

T

**is for tree,
rooted safe in the ground.**

To write the letter T the Egyptians used a loaf of bread. To spell **tree**
using hieroglyphs, you would write

t r e e.

Good wood for making things was hard to find in ancient Egypt.
That's why they built their houses out of sun-dried mud bricks.

U

**is for unravelling
the secret of hieroglyphs.**

To write the letter U the Egyptians used a quail chick. To spell
unravel using hieroglyphs, you would write

u n r a v e l.

The Egyptians wrote on long sheets of papyrus and then rolled them
up. The scroll this man is reading says "love."

V

**is for vulture
who soars from the cliffs.**

The Egyptians had no letter V, but you can use a horned viper (f) for the V sound. To spell **vulture**, write

v u l t u r e.

Many birds were worshipped as symbols of the gods. The vulture, the falcon and the ibis were some of them.

V

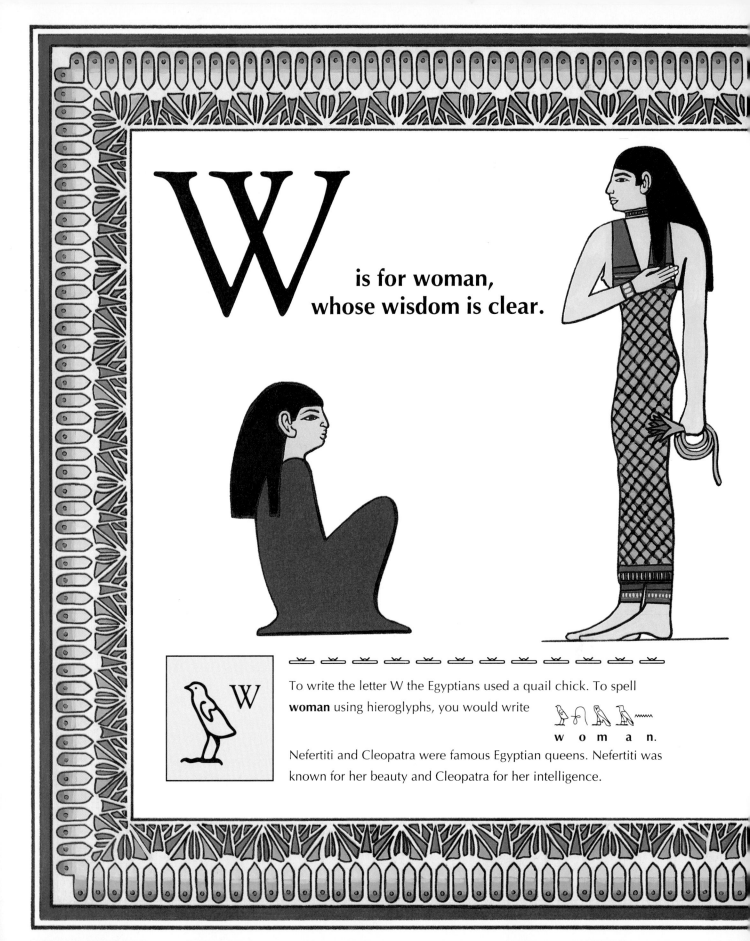

W

**is for woman,
whose wisdom is clear.**

To write the letter W the Egyptians used a quail chick. To spell **woman** using hieroglyphs, you would write

w o m a n.

Nefertiti and Cleopatra were famous Egyptian queens. Nefertiti was known for her beauty and Cleopatra for her intelligence.

X

**marks the spot
because you are here.**

The Egyptians had no letter X, but you can use a basket (k) and a folded cloth (s) instead. To spell **six**, you would write

s i x.

The big round hieroglyph above shows two streets crossing each other. The Egyptians had both large cities and small villages.

X

**is for youth,
a young girl or boy.**

To write the letter Y the Egyptians used two reed leaves. To spell **youth** using hieroglyphs, you would write

y o u t h.

The finger raised toward the mouth is the Egyptian way to show a young person. Many kids had shaved heads, with one lock of hair on the side, called a side-lock.

Y

Z

**is for zoo—
a place of great joy!**

To write the letter Z the Egyptians used a door bolt. To spell **zoo**, you would write

z o o.

The Egyptians had many signs for animals, and they even had zoos too! Animals were brought from North Africa, the Near East and the Red Sea Coast.

Z

What's a Hieroglyph Anyway?

Long ago—over 5,000 years ago—the ancient Egyptians found a way to put their spoken language into writing. At first, the Egyptians used pictures to record their words and ideas. For example, they used a ⊙ to stand for the word "sun."

As they needed to write down more and more complicated ideas, their language grew and changed. The ⊙ was a good way to represent "sun," but how would you say "sunny day" or "sunspot" or "sunburn"? Instead of coming up with new pictures for these new ideas, the Egyptians combined one hieroglyph with another hieroglyph to create new words.

Here's an example of this idea:

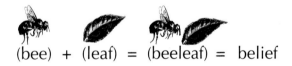

(bee) + (leaf) = (beeleaf) = belief

So in addition to being pictures, hieroglyphs were also sounds. With time, the Egyptians started combining one sound with another sound to make words.

We do the same thing in English. We have twenty-six letters in our alphabet that represent many different sounds. We combine these to make words. The ancient Egyptians had hundreds of different hiero-glyphs, and they combined them to make words.

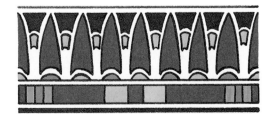

When explorers first began to investigate the ancient pyramids and temples of Egypt, they found mummies, statues and monuments covered with beautiful hieroglyphs. But no one understood what they said. They thought that hieroglyphs must be secret coded magical spells!

It was only in 1822, after years of studying the famous Rosetta Stone, that a Frenchman named Jean-Francois Champollion finally cracked the code. This stone, discovered by Napoleon's army in 1799, contained one royal inscription in three different languages: one form of Greek and two forms of Egyptian. Since Greek was still understood, Champollion compared it to the ancient Egyptian in order to decipher the language of the pharaohs. That wasn't all that long ago!

The Egyptians used hieroglyphs to write letters and stories. They used them to decorate tombs and temple walls. They carved them on large stones in order to record the words and orders of their kings. And they used them to figure taxes, and to compose songs and hymns.

Not everyone knew how to write in hieroglyphs. Only very few Egyptians were sent to school. Most of the people were busy raising crops for food. A small group of people—the scribes, priests and administrators—did the reading and writing for everyone. They kept tax accounts, wrote letters, kept records of trials, and read the royal decrees.

Hieroglyphs were often written in red and black ink on papyrus. Papyrus plants had long stalks. By cutting the dry stalks into thin strips and weaving them together, the Egyptians created a form of ancient paper. And instead of pencils they wrote with reed pens, which they dipped in ink.

Hieroglyphs were also carved and painted on tomb and temple walls. Often many people were involved in the creation of these hieroglyphs, and it could take months to finish the decoration. First a draftsman would draw the hieroglyphs. Then a sculptor would carve the outlines. Finally, other artisans would paint the hieroglyphs. The colors of the hieroglyphs in this book were carefully chosen to match the colors that the ancient Egyptians used.

As time passed, people from different cultures came to Egypt, and they brought different customs and different languages. Slowly, the Egyptians began to write their language with the Greek alphabet, which was simpler to use, and only the priests in the temples continued to write in beautiful hieroglyphs. The last hieroglyphic inscription we know of dates to the year 394 A.D.

Write Your Own Secret Messages!

We've included a stencil with this book so you, too, can write in hieroglyphs. All you have to do is punch the hieroglyph shapes out of the cardboard. Once you do this, you have a choice: you can trace around the inside of the hieroglyph hole you have created, or you can trace around the outside of the hieroglyph shape you punched out.

When we write in English, we write in one direction, from left to right. But hieroglyphs can be written in three different directions: from left to right (like English); from right to left (like Arabic and Hebrew); and from top to bottom (like Chinese). How do you know which way to read? Look at the hieroglyphs of people or animals, and look into their faces. Read into their faces, as though you were talking to them.

For example, take a look at the lion in HELLO.

When you use the stencils to write words and messages, you can turn them over if you want to write in the other direction.

The ancient Egyptian language is not only complex, it is beautiful. Scribes tried very hard to make hieroglyphs look balanced and well-spaced. They didn't always write in a straight line as we do. If two small or skinny hieroglyphs were next to each other in a word, they were put together to make them look better. Using the same example as above, the Egyptians would have written HELLO like this:

On the next two pages, you will find a chart of the hieroglyphs in **A** through **Z** order. The first column shows the Egyptian hieroglyph. The second column shows which letter it matches in the English alphabet. The third column shows what the hieroglyph sounds like. The last column tells you what the hieroglyph is a picture of.

The Egyptians had many letters and sounds that we do not have in our English alphabet. And we have many letters and sounds that the ancient Egyptians didn't have. As you read through this book, you noticed that there are no hieroglyphs for C, U, V and X.

In English, we know C can have a "hard" or "soft" sound—it can sound like "s" as in cent, or "k" as in car. For U you would use the W hieroglyph. For V you would use the F hieroglyph. And because X sounds like the "ks" sound in "licks" you would use two hieroglyphs together—the K and the S. We've pointed you to the right hieroglyph to use based on the *sound* it makes.

See if you can read this paragraph:

[hieroglyphs] you have a [hieroglyphs] day [hieroglyphs] ?
We [hieroglyphs] you have [hieroglyphs] with this [hieroglyphs] .

Now that you know some of the secrets of this mysterious language, you can try it yourself!

HIEROGLYPH	LETTER	AS IN THE WORD	OBJECT SHOWN
	A	apple, Andy	vulture
	B	boy, Bob	foot
	C	cat, Cathy	basket
	C	cent, Cindy	folded cloth
	CH	cheese, Chuck	rope
	D	dog, Denise	hand
	E	end, Emily	reed leaf
	F	fun, Frank	horned viper
	G	go, Gary	pot stand
	H	hat, Helen	shelter
	I	in, Isabelle	reed leaf
	J	joke, Julie	snake
	K	kite, Karen	basket
	L	like, Lucy	lion

HIEROGLYPH	LETTER	AS IN THE WORD	OBJECT SHOWN
🦉	M	man, Mike	owl
〜〜〜	N	nose, Nancy	water
	O	open, Omar	lasso
▢	P	pen, Peter	stool
◁	Q	quick, Quentin	hill
⬯	R	rose, Ruby	mouth
|	S	sun, Sandy	folded cloth
⌓	T	toes, Terry	loaf of bread
🐦	U	uncle, Ursula	quail chick
	V	very, Victor	horned viper
🐦	W	wall, Wendy	quail chick
⌣ |	X	X-ray, Xavier	basket + folded cloth
⑂⑂ , \\\\	Y	yes, Yolanda	2 reed leaves, or 2 strokes
⊶	Z	zoo, Zachary	door bolt

About the Author

Peter Der Manuelian became interested in ancient Egypt not long after learning his own ABCs. He received a B.A. in Near Eastern Languages and Civilizations from Harvard University and a Ph.D. in Egyptology from the University of Chicago. After working at the Pyramids of Giza and the temples of Thebes in Egypt, he joined the curatorial staff of the Department of Egyptian and Ancient Near Eastern Art of the Museum of Fine Arts, Boston. He is interested in using the tools of the future to study the past, and combined his hand-drawn hieroglyphic artwork with a computer to produce this book.

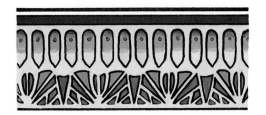

Some Thank You's

I would like to thank Rus Gant for providing photographs on which some of the drawings are based. Cleo Huggins designed the hieroglyphic computer typeface that appears at the bottom of the pages, and Dexter Sear assisted in converting these designs to a keyboard font. Their work has greatly enhanced this one. Suwin Chan created the cover painting, the border art, and added color to my line drawings. Janet O'Donoghue and the late Boston artist, Olga Sears, made numerous suggestions to the layout of the manuscript. All these friends have my heartfelt thanks. Most importantly, Kathryn Sky-Peck and Gisela Voss, both of the Museum of Fine Arts, Boston, expertly oversaw the design and production. Their energy, creativity and vision turned this book into a reality.

"Its beginning
has come
to its end,
as it was found
in writing."

This phrase usually comes at the end of ancient Egyptian stories written on papyrus. It means:

"THE END"